NTD 2

GLENN SPRUNGER

TABLE OF CONTENTS

Table of Contents

WELCOME

An invitation to develop deep roots and relationships

Discipleship matters to God because He desires to transform us into wholehearted disciple-makers. We don't grow in a vacuum. Instead, God designed us to come and grow together into His likeness. You now have a cutting-edge communication tool to sharpen and to prepare you for high-impact ministry. You get to decide what to do with it.

Welcome to NTD 2 - the second of three triathlon discipleship courses to build your spiritual fitness and to prepare you for the 90-Day Cross Training Adventure. NTD 2 is a small-group discipleship tool designed to facilitate heart-felt discussions with your spiritual family and friends about significant relationship issues.

In his letter to the church at Ephesus, the Apostle Paul wrote a letter of encouragement to his spiritual friends who believed in Jesus Christ. As you read and study together Paul's letter to the Ephesians, my prayer is that you will experience and share the love, peace, and joy that comes from deeply knowing Jesus Christ and from becoming more deeply engaged in spiritual friendships.

Paul painted two word-pictures for the Christian community to explore: a tree with deep roots and a house with a strong foundation. People and relationships become healthier and stronger when they are deeply-rooted in God's enduring love. When Jesus Christ becomes the foundation of our lives, God builds us into a spiritual family and community to reflect His glory and truth to the world.

As you digest, learn, and apply God's definition of who you are in Christ, you will be growing the root system for a secure identity. Part of the process of strengthening the growing believer's identity will be meeting together on a weekly basis, studying God's truths found in Scripture, speaking and praying those truths into one another's lives, and finding

Welcome

practical ways to affirm and apply these truths in daily living. In order to grow together as a spiritual family, we must prioritize and commit our lives to making time and room for connecting with one another throughout the week as we celebrate victories together and fight spiritual battles together. Spiritual families and friendships only grow strong and endure as we faithfully pray for and stay connected to one another.

While *NTD 1* was written for seekers and young believers to develop tools to understand and apply Scripture to daily living, *NTD 2 is a New Testament Discipleship course for people who long to live in spiritual community* but are not sure how to move from "going to church together" to "living in community together." If you are looking for a group where you can fully engage yourself with other disciples of Jesus who are hungry to be known and loved in community, then NTD 2 may be just the group for you.

The duration of your NTD 2 group may vary in time depending on how seriously you take God's words and apply them to your lives and relationships. Christian discipleship is not measured by how fast you conquer a book. Instead, it is measured by how well our lives, relationships, and community are informed, reformed, and transformed by the words we read together, understand, and apply from Scripture. I recommend using the New Living Translation (NLT) with NTD 2. Take your time as you move together through the written material and discussion questions in your NTD 2 manual. You will notice that most groups have "internal" and "external" processors. Please be patient with the people in your group who think too much and those who talk too much. Make room to enjoy and encourage the differences and strengths of one another.

As you allow God's Spirit to grow and change you as a group of Christ-followers, remember that you are God's masterpieces, a group of people God chose long ago to form a community where His Spirit enables you to do the good things He planned long ago for you to do.

Glenn Sprunger

Ephesians 1:1-14

Showered with Kindness

Leader: As we move as a group into a new season of exploring God's Word together, we'll begin with a metaphor from your kitchen or from your favorite restaurant.

- What will happen if you add some extra coffee in your filter as you brew your favorite blend of coffee for you to enjoy drinking with your friends?

- What will happen if you keep your tea bag dipped in your hot water for some extra time before you enjoy drinking tea with your friends?

As we come together expecting God to speak into our lives and into our relationships, our study will be stronger and richer if we allow some extra time to share observations and questions, to take a phrase-at-a-time, and to apply the words to our lives and relationships. We will need the Holy Spirit to lead us, so let's begin each group asking for His guidance. *(Allow time for group members to pray together.)*

Facilitator:

- Have you ever been through an adoption process with someone?

- Adoption can be a lengthy, complicated, and expensive process. What are some of the stages that families go through before, during, and after an adoption?

- Can you remember a season of your life when things were rough in your family and you secretly thought to yourself, "Wow, I wish I was part of a different family?"

1

Ephesians 1:1-14

Reader: Let's go around the group and read together a story about God's amazing adoption plan found in Ephesians 1:1-14.

Now let's read in unison God's plan for each of our lives.

"His unchanging plan has always been to adopt us into His own family by bringing us to Himself through Jesus Christ. And this gave Him great pleasure" (Ephesians 1:5 NLT).

Leader: Have you ever talked with a family member or a relative who reflected way back to times before you were even born? In his profound letter to the Ephesians, Paul takes us "waaaaaay" back to our Designer, the One who planned out our lives before He even created this world and long before He gave us our first breath.

The Designer, our Adoptive Father, painted a beautiful word picture for us to experience and enjoy. God loved us and chose us to be the recipients of His spiritual blessing. Picture God pouring out His wonderful kindness upon us by purchasing our freedom through the blood of Christ and by forgiving our sins. He showers us with wisdom and understanding. While God is smiling from ear-to-ear, we realize that we are loved and chosen by God, and we are completely free from the penalty of our sins. We are now His own children. We now belong, and we have a Christ-centered identity. And to prove it, God has sealed us with His Holy Spirit, guaranteeing our identity and our inheritance from God. We belong to His dearly-loved Son!

Facilitator: Go ahead and draw what you pictured in your mind as you heard these words. *(Remember to provide paper, drawing materials, and unhurried time. You get to create a safe space for the Holy Spirit to work in, through, and between us. Be prepared for the diversity of expressions that unfold. The artists will be all over this opportunity. Some of your left-brained people may want to make this a completely-cognitive experience. Some may feel self-conscious and say, "I can't draw." Some may experience anxiety and want to fill the room with words and to interrupt the work of the Spirit in the hearts of your group members. You may want to turn on some quiet, soothing music to help create a peaceful, safe space for people to create.*

You may also feel pressure to over-function and create something for others to see or experience. Just relax and let the Holy Spirit lead. All of the internal and external dynamics of your group will likely "hit-the-fan" during this initial opportunity to creatively process God's Word. Some people in your group may have never even thought of drawing God's Word-pictures that we find throughout Scripture. Relax and trust God and the people He brought into your life and group experience.)

- As you are drawing this Biblical word-picture, how is the Holy Spirit expanding your concept of God?

- How will this word-picture impact how you see and understand and relate to yourself?

- What impact would you like it have on how you see and relate to one another?

- When do you need a shower of kindness reminding you that you belong, you are loved, you are His, and that God is delighted with you?

- What are some of the reasons why you hold back from showering people with God's kindness and love?

- What was this first NTD 2 group like for you?

- Name one thing you learned today about God, yourself, or someone in our group.

- What is one way you hope to apply something you have learned from our group today?

Leader: Today you were introduced to some mind, life, and relationship-altering truths that can change you. They'll need some time to sink in. If you allow yourself and the Holy Spirit time this week to sit with the words and images and connections in this passage, the Holy Spirit may lead you to know and experience what's been desperately missing and needed in your life. Here's your personal invitation and challenge.

TAKING THE NTD CHALLENGE

NTD level 1 challenge: Carve out time this week to just sit with this text. Unclutter your mind. Anticipate the words and truths of this passage to collide with some of your limited understanding of God, yourself, and people. Don't be surprised if the Holy Spirit begins to do some house-cleaning. Some of your internalized images and messages may collide with the eternal truths that you will be introduced to in this initial part of your NTD 2 experience. Don't shrink back from spiritual challenges by rejecting what your mind has trouble grasping.

NTD level 2 challenge: Expand your understanding of this initial passage in Ephesians by looking up some of the related biblical texts that will help unpack its meaning. Genesis 1. 1 Peter 1:20. James 1:5. Jeremiah 9:23-24. Philippians 2:9-11. Galatians 4:3-7.

NTD level 3 challenge: Take a pen and a highlighter, and circle or underline the names and words you find below each time you see them in this passage. Begin drawing or making mental and spiritual connections each time these words are found or mentioned in this Ephesians 1:1-14 NLT passage. Anticipate the Holy Spirit breaking into your experience to teach you and to give you new insights.

- "Jesus Christ"
- "belong"
- "long ago"
- "kindness"
- "praise"
- "plan"

Closing Prayer: Lord, Help us to "live in" and "live out" a Christ-centered worldview that leads us to sing in the shower, smile in the mirror, smile and encourage one another, and offer as a group the love of Christ that our world desperately needs to feel. Amen.

Ephesians 1:15-23

Flooded with Light, Power, and Presence

Leader: There is an old children's song by Bill & Gloria Gaither with a catchy tune that affirms God's truth about each of us. *"I am a promise. I am a possibility. I am a promise with a capital 'P'. I am a great big bundle of potentiality. And I am learning to hear God's voice, and I am trying to make the right choices. I am a promise to be everything God wants me to be"* (Gaither). But instead of singing songs of hope and of living in light of God's promises, we get bogged down by the cares of this world, and we lose our focus, our light, our song, our strength, and our joy. Wasted potential, unfulfilled dreams, fractured relationships, fatigue, loneliness, and frustration may better describe the person you see in the mirror.

Our knee-jerk reaction may be to quickly say, "Not me! I have a good life." But when was the last time that you heard people talking about your strong faith or your strong love for people everywhere? As we scroll back through the archives of the early church in Ephesus, we may discover a strength of faith and a depth of love for one another that we desperately need in our church today.

If you are a person of prayer or someone who needs to write things down so that you do not forget to do something important, get out your pen or highlighter as we explore the prayer life of a prayer warrior who penned his prayer to the church at Ephesus. Let's go around the group and read together Ephesians 1:15-23.

Facilitator: As we unpack Paul's prayer together,

- What words or phrases caught your attention?

- Let's work together and write down all of the things that Paul asked God for in his prayer for the church?

5

Ephesians 1:15-23

_____

_____

_____

_____

_____

_____

- How many of these "prayer requests" are part of your daily prayer for the church?

- What is one thing that you want to add to your prayer life as you are learning from Paul's prayer life?

Leader: Imagine going to church on Sunday morning, closing your eyes, bowing your head to pray, and hearing the pastor begin his prayer by asking God to give you spiritual wisdom so that you can know and understand God. Then all of a sudden, you are flooded with a bright picture of your future as a church. You get a super-surge of God's resurrection power, and you are overwhelmed by God's presence in this place. As you open your eyes, your pastor informs you that every day he prays, in unison with Jesus, this prayer over you. How would you feel?

How easy it is to stop praying for the church. How easy it is to forget that Jesus is interceding on our behalf for God's will to be done on earth as it is in heaven. How frequently we spend money to remodel or rewire our homes, but we do not spend much time praying for God's power in and through the church.

Facilitator: When was the last time you...

- Were overwhelmed by God's presence and power in your life?

- Prayed consistently for your church?

- Were so impressed by someone's faith and love that you gave thanks to God for them?

6

Leader: As we look to Scripture as a pattern to guide our prayer life as a group, may we commit to pray this short prayer each day over each of the members of our group and watch what God does over the next week.

Father, I thank you for _____. I will keep asking you to give _____ the spirit of wisdom and revelation to know You better, to see and know Your hope, and to experience Your power and presence throughout this day. Amen.

Ephesians 1:15-23

Ephesians 2:1-10
Saved by Grace

Facilitator: As we begin our group, let's discuss what it was like praying for one another over the past week. *(pause)* Let's make some time right now to pray together. *(pray)*

- As you reflect back on your life, who comes to your mind as a person who showed you God's unconditional love? What did they say and do that helped you to feel loved just the way you are?

- Do you spend more time thinking about what's right with you or what's wrong with you?

Leader: God, the great lover of our souls, demonstrated His unconditional, great love to us, right in the middle of our great sinning, by offering us a new life of love and grace. Let's read together God's marvelous love story in Ephesians 2:1-10.

When you get together with your old friends or with your family, are you more likely to hear them telling good stories or bad stories about your life? *(pause)* As we begin to reflect on the first three verses of our "God story" from Ephesians 2, we share the same history. We became quite skilled at sinning, and Paul was just telling it like it <u>is</u>. Or was Paul telling it like it <u>was</u>? If you look carefully, the first three verses were all written in the past tense. In the NLT, we discover an honest but sad commentary of our history.

"Once you were dead, doomed forever because of your many sins. You used to live just like the rest of the world, full of sin, obeying Satan" (v. 1-2).

9

Ephesians 2:1-10

But as we transition to verses 4 and 5, our sad, dead story gets revived as we are introduced to our loving, merciful God who graced us and saved us through His Son, Jesus Christ. We all needed to "get a life", and He gave us a new one. Not only did God revive us from our spiritual deadness to sin, but He also gave us a new position - ***"being seated with Him in the heavenly realms"*** (v. 5, 6).

The curious ones in the group may wonder, "How could He love us this way" when He knew how much that we have sinned against Him? Others may wonder, "Why He did do this?" Fortunately, we are given the answers to some of our questions, though we may not fully understand God's love, grace, and mercy. Why are seasoned, saved sinners positioned with Christ in the heavenly realms? Paul gave us two answers:

1. ***"All because we are one with Christ Jesus"*** (v. 6).

2. ***"And so God can always point to us as examples of the incredible wealth of His favor and kindness toward us, as shown in all He has done for us through Christ Jesus"*** (v. 7).

Facilitator: Some of the words and pictures that we are shown in this passage may seem too good to be true.

- What is difficult for you to *understand* as you reflect on God's words penned by Paul?

- What is difficult for you to *accept* about God's special favor for you? Have you ever felt "favored" before?

- What is the difference between our physical, human condition and our spiritual position?

- How does your current "God-image" affect your current "self-image?"

- How will these words recorded in Scripture change or improve how you see God, yourself, and one another?

10

Leader: Let's read together Ephesians 2:8-10. If we add these three verses to what we know from our study of Scripture, we are developing a strong root system for a Christ-centered identity. The seven foundational truths that you are about to digest may be quite different from what you were told or shown in your past. But these truths will form roots for your identity that are deeply connected to the God who designed you for His purposes.

We have been:

1. Created in the loving, good image of God, and what God designed is good (Genesis 1:27,31).

2. Shaped by the hands of God, and we are safely held in God's hands (Job 10:8, 12:10).

3. Fearfully and wonderfully made, our days have been ordained by our ever-present God (Psalm 139).

4. Loved and chosen by God, before He made the world, to be holy and without fault in His eyes through Christ (Eph. 1:4).

We who believe have been:

5. Adopted into God's family, sealed by the Holy Spirit, guaranteeing that we are His own children (Eph. 1:5, 14).

6. Saved by grace when we believed and received God's free gift of salvation based on His love and grace (2:8,9).

7. Made as God's masterpiece, created anew in Jesus Christ to do the good things He planned for us long ago (2:10).

Facilitator:

• How closely does your identity and self-image align with these Bible-based truths?

- How often is your view of other Christians based on these Biblical foundations?

Brennan Manning, author of *A Glimpse of Jesus: The Stranger to Self-Hatred*, believes that people will not accept that their lives are valuable to God unless someone demonstrates this to them in real-life relationships. According to Manning, *"The Christian's warmth and congeniality, nonjudgmental attitude, and welcoming love may well be the catalyst allowing the healing power of Jesus to become operative in the life of an alienated, forlorn brother or sister"* (Manning 65).

- What is your reaction to these statements?

- Where are you in the process of understanding, accepting, and expressing God's love and grace?

- What are some practical ways that you show people that they are valuable to God and to you?

We are living in a time where most people are struggling with some form of an addiction. We are trying to do something to make us feel good about ourselves or to get someone else to feel good about us. We try performance, people-pleasing, working longer and harder, looking better, pornography, gambling, alcohol and drugs, making more money, buying more, knowing more, video games, social media, and even using sports, pleasures, and hobbies. It is no wonder that people have a hard time digesting these simple words: ***"God saved you by His special favor when you believed"*** (v. 8). Yes, all it takes is a little faith. And to make sure that we understand this, God added: ***"And you cannot take credit for this; it is a gift from God. Salvation is not a reward for the good things we have done, so none of us can boast about it"*** (v. 9-10).

- What comes to your mind when you hear God, your Designer, say, ***"For we are God's masterpiece?"*** (v. 10) *(pause for discussion)* Ron Hutchcraft, in his teaching in his book *5 Needs Your Child Must Have Met at Home*, said that we are like fine china, set apart for God's special purpose and for special occasions (Hutchcraft 47). Others have tried to define "masterpiece" by saying that God determined our value by the price He paid for our lives. In other words, God determined that we have great value in His eyes, and we cannot change, add to, or subtract from our God-given value.

- We have much to learn about God, our value, and how to value one another. Our group can be a place where we learn and demonstrate our value to God and to one another. To help in this process, let's go around the group and complete this sentence: "I will feel valued by this group when you…"

- Is it easier for you to validate people or invalidate people? Why?

- In order for me to trust you and allow you to play an active role in helping me feel rooted in God's love, I will need to _____, and I will need you to _____.

"Trust is the courage to accept acceptance." --Paul Tillich (Manning 102)

"I am lovable because He loves me. Period." --Brennan Manning (Manning 88)

TAKING THE NTD CHALLENGE

Your **NTD Take-Home Challenge** is to prayerfully invest time exploring with God His answer to this question: *"Long ago, what good things did You design me to do?"* Together you may begin to complete this sentence: "I'm God's masterpiece, and He created me to _____."

Prayer: Father, We thank You for sending Your Son, Jesus Christ, to save us by Your grace and to make us new. Set us free from our old way of seeing ourselves. Give us Your progressive vision to see ourselves and to see one another the way You see us. Sanctify our imaginations so that

Ephesians 2:1-10

we can begin to see the good things that You planned long ago for us to do. Give us courage to move forward boldly and gracefully in the power of Your Spirit saying and doing exactly what You made us for. In Jesus' Name we ask and pray. Amen.

Ephesians 2:11-22
Removing the Barriers

Facilitator: Let's begin our group with prayer. *(pause)* We're going to take some time to reflect on our lives and share some of our life stories as we respond to these questions:

- What comes to your mind when you think about your life *before* you became a Christian?

- What are some *names* that people called you?

- Talk about a time when you felt excluded or left out or didn't fit in *at church*.

- How easy is it to *exclude non-Christians* from your daily or weekly routine?

- How much are we actually *including one another* in our daily and weekly experiences?

- What *barriers* do each of us still have in our lives that keep us from living in Christian community with one another? Is it okay to talk about it?

As we read together Ephesians 2:11-18, we'll make time for each of us:

- To share something that caught our attention.

- To discuss as a group what it means.

- And to explore the potential impact it may make on how we do relationships.

Leader: From reading this passage, it is obvious that we are not the first group of Christians who has ever judged or alienated another group of

15

Ephesians 2:11-22

Christians. We have a long history of dividing into groups and creating barriers that separate us.

What "separated" and set apart Jewish Christians from Gentile Christians was circumcision, although their circumcision made no impact on the hearts of the Jews.

We might be quick to judge some of the Jews who thought that they were privileged and superior to the Gentile Christians. But I wonder *how much of our hearts and lives and relationships are not yet affected by our Christianity.*

Keep in mind that Paul's letter to the Ephesians was written primarily to a group of Gentile Christians. Not only did Paul remind them of their hopeless former life of being far from God and excluded from the faith community, but he also reminded them that they now belong to Christ Jesus. What kept them apart had been destroyed, and now they were close to Christ because of His blood shed for them on the cross.

The good news is that Jesus didn't stop there. Jesus didn't just come to "make peace" between Himself and His children. Jesus came to destroy our personal, spiritual, and relational barriers that stood between one another in the church. He terminated the whole system and problem of excluding people in and from God's family. The walls of hostility that separated people were broken down and destroyed by Jesus. Jesus, our peace, reconciled us and made us into one group, His family. Now we all may freely come to God through the Holy Spirit as a result of Jesus' completed work on the cross and through His glorious resurrection.

Facilitator: Now we get to slow down and reflect on how we are doing at allowing these truths to affect our lives.

- Are we living at peace with one another in our family?

- Are we living at peace with one another in our group?

- Are we living at peace with one another in the Church?

- What barriers must be removed between us for us to live at peace and to live in community with each other?

- How would you complete this sentence: "Most people in this group do not understand why I _____."

Leader: The conclusion of this second chapter of Ephesians clearly defines for Christians who we are and whose we are. These foundational truths will provide each of us with a secure foundation and a secure home from which we can live and share life with one another. Let's read together Ephesians 2:19-22. Now let's read together these formative truths.

We who believe are:

- Citizens and members of God's family (2:19).

- God's house built and founded upon His prophets, apostles, and Jesus Christ, the Cornerstone of our home (2:20).

- Carefully joined together to become a temple where God's Spirit dwells (2:21,22).

TAKING THE NTD CHALLENGE

Please choose which challenge(s) you are ready for and lean into those challenge(s).

NTD level 1 challenge: Members of healthy, growing families make time to share meals together. Your challenge is to schedule a time for your NTD 2 family to come together for a shared meal. Work together to plan out all the details, and enjoy some good food and fellowship together. Warning: You may enjoy this and make an ongoing habit of eating together.

Ephesians 2:11-22

NTD level 2 challenge: To help your identity become more deeply rooted in God and His truths found in Scripture, take a pair of scissors and cut out the 10 Christ-centered identity statements found in our last two sessions. For those who frequently raid the refrigerator at home, place these 10 statements on the refrigerator. For those who spend more time in front of the mirror in the morning, tape these 10 statements to the mirror. For those who watch lots of TV, tape them to the TV. For those who travel a lot, tape them in your vehicle. For those who spend a lot of time on the computer, tape them around your screen. Then allow yourself to meditate on these truths each day, and watch what happens to your relationships with God, yourself, and others.

NTD level 3 challenge: Spend some extended time with your NTD 2 group discussing how your relationships with one another will be different because Christ is your foundation and because of the truths you have learned from Scripture. How will people who are *"carefully joined together to become a dwelling place for God's Spirit"* (v. 21) talk and act towards one another and towards those who witness our group? We are God's family. We're sons and daughters of the Most High God. We're brothers and sisters in one family - God's family. If you need some guidance for this challenge, look up and discuss Ephesians 4:29, 31.

"Outside-the-box" challenge: For the creative, spirited, or trendsetting people in your group, take the words you have just studied from Ephesians 1 and 2 and develop your own unique challenge that will help you put into practice what you are learning.

Lean into your challenge and watch what God does!

Ephesians 3:1-13

Sharing the Secret

Leader: Secrets are part of our personal lives. They represent significant truths that we share with only those whom we trust. We test people out to find out if they can be trusted with different parts of our lives. And when people have been confidential and trustworthy, we begin to share more and more "secrets" from our lives in hopes that we will be known and loved. On the other hand, if people violate our trust, we find our world feeling "less safe," and we may begin to shut down some and shrink our world and the freedom we may once have felt to share our lives with others.

Facilitator:

- What came to your mind when you started thinking about trying to trust people with secrets?

- What do you look for in a *friend* that you can trust?

- What *qualities* do you look for in a *small group* of spiritual friends who will help you to feel safe enough to let people know you for who you really are?

- What are some experiences you have had that make it hard to open up and trust people with the real you?

- Have you noticed some patterns in our group that *encourage or discourage* you from sharing more of your thoughts, feelings, experiences, questions, and convictions?

Leader: Let's read together Ephesians 3:1-13. Can you imagine what it must have been like for the Apostle Paul to be the carrier of God's secret plan that the world had been searching for? Now you may think that there have been some things you have said and done in your past that would keep you from being used by God. But Paul's life story illustrates that *God uses unlikely characters to become vessels through which His Spirit moves and speaks.*

God took a man who persecuted Christians and made him into a man who proclaimed God's secret plan and God's favor to marginalized Christians. His message was this: because of God's big heart and Christ's sacrificial death on the cross, you have an equal share in God's blessings and an amazing inheritance.

Not only did Paul not deserve this wonderful privilege to proclaim God's plan and blessings, but we also do not deserve the grace and blessings that we have through Christ. God gave His grace and blessings to us because He loves us and because we need it. God trusted Paul with His secret plan, and He also trusts us with the secret! It is the best secret that you could ever keep, and it is the best secret for us to share.

Did you get a sense of prisoner Paul's excitement and passion as he penned these words for the church? Three times he repeated the word *"special"* (Ephesians 3:2, 7, 8). He was a thankful recipient of a *special* ministry, having received God's *special* favor, to glow with a *special* joy of telling the Gentiles of the endless treasures available to them through Christ.

Facilitator:

- When was the last time you were so *overjoyed* with God's good news that you had to write or tell someone about it?

- What *cause* do you feel so strongly about that you would risk your life or risk going to jail because you stand up for it?

- What *special ministry* do you think that God is preparing you to do?

- When does *God's plan* for your life feel like a secret or like a mystery to you?

Leader: The impact of this passage of Scripture must have built encouragement, comfort, unity, and confidence in the church in Ephesus. Because of Christ and their faith in Christ, there was nothing to separate the church from God, and nothing to separate people of diverse backgrounds from one another. The church of Ephesus could join their faith and hearts with Paul and say:

"Because of Christ and our faith in Him, we can now come fearlessly into God's presence, assured of His glad welcome" (Ephesians 3:12).

But I wonder if we come *boldly* to God today *with confidence* of His open arms and grace. Do we come together in faith with people from different backgrounds and *confidently* approach God's throne, expecting Him to *hear* us and to *respond gladly* to our praise and to our requests?

Facilitator: Let's take some time to respond to these questions and the responses of our group members. *(pause)*

Since Christ has destroyed the barriers that caused separation between God and His people and the barriers that once separated God's people from one another,

- How freely do you *come to God* after you have failed or sinned?

- How freely do you *come to God's people* around you and share your hopes, dreams, fears, faults, secrets, frustrations, needs, and desires?

- How freely do you pray with and for the people in our group?

- Can you identify one barrier that God has helped you to overcome in building your trust and faith?

- Can you identify one barrier that you will need some help removing in order for you to trust God and people more freely?

21

Ephesians 3:1-13

Prayer: Let's close our group with each of us praying a short prayer for someone in our group.

Ephesians 3:14-21
Rooted Prayer

Leader: I want you to imagine that you wake up one morning with an urgent desire to pray. You get out of bed and fall to your knees. And without any forewarning, you have a mind that is completely full of the wisdom of God. Then you notice that your heart feels differently. When you tune into your heart, you are in awe when you recognize that God transplanted His heart into your heart while you were sleeping. Your mind and heart are completely in sync with God's mind and heart, and now it is time to pray.

- What do you imagine that you would be praying for? *(pause)*

Let's read together in Ephesians 3:14-21 Paul's prayer for his spiritual friends.

When Paul got a glimpse of God's wisdom and master plan for His creation, he was driven to his knees to pray. He prayed to the Father, the One who created, defined, and named us.

Facilitator: Let's take time to unpack and respond to each phrase of this prayer.

"I pray that from His glorious, unlimited resources He will give you mighty inner strength through His Holy Spirit" (v. 16).

"And I pray that Christ will be more and more at home in your hearts as you trust in Him" (v. 17a).

"May your roots go down deep into the soil of God's marvelous love" (v. 17b).

Ephesians 3:14-21

"And may you have the power to understand, as all God's people should, how wide, how long, how high, and how deep His love really is" (v. 18).

"May you experience the love of Christ, though it is so great you will never fully understand it" (v. 19a).

"Then you will be filled with the fullness of life and power that comes from God" (v. 19b).

"Now glory be to God! By His mighty power at work within us, He is able to accomplish infinitely more than we would ever dare to ask or hope" (v. 20).

"May He be given glory in the church and in Christ Jesus forever and ever through endless ages. Amen" (v. 21).

Leader: Paul approached God with freedom and confidence. Fully convinced of all that he knew to be true about who God is and who he was, Paul asked God to pass on the fullness of His love and His power to the root system and identity of his friends so that they, too, could feel and know and be filled with the life and power that comes from God.

When our *identity* becomes deeply rooted in God and in His marvelous, infinite love, God gives us the heart and desire for those around us to become anchored in the fullness of God's love. But this identity reformation can be a long and painful process.

When our identity is securely attached to a false sense of security or to something that we can lose, God may initiate a long and painful process of uprooting us and removing the old root system and replacing it with a solid, secure root system. If you need some identity root work done so that your relationship with God and with people can be healthier, will you allow God and your NTD 2 group to help you through this process? *(pause for reflection time)*

Facilitator: Which of these *"old root systems"* have organized you at some point in your life?

- *PROTECTION FIRST!* Trying to control situations and people so that no one, including myself, gets hurt.

- *PEOPLE FIRST!* Striving to do all that I can to make sure that those around me get what they need, get what they want, so that they feel good, and so that they don't get mad at me.

- *PLEASURE FIRST!* Living each day with the goal of doing things that make me feel good, and avoiding people and situations that make me feel badly.

- *POSITION FIRST!* Making sure that I am in a place and role and position where I am comfortable and confident and less likely to feel insecure or risk failure.

- *PERFORMANCE FIRST!* Always working harder and doing my best at everything because it makes me feel good, and other people count on me to always work hard, to look good, or to do my best.

- *POSSESSIONS FIRST!* Striving to make more money and to buy newer, bigger, or more things that help me to feel good about myself.

- *POWER FIRST!* Striving to control and manipulate people and situations so that I get what I want and avoid feeling dependent, weak, needy, or out of control.

- *PERFECTION FIRST!* Doing everything myself and making sure it is done "right," even though I am worn out from striving. Everyone else is having more fun, and I do not try new things because I might fail. At least I do not have to trust other people who could mess it up.

- *PUMP UP FIRST!* Making sure that I am physically fit, strong, and healthy. Exercising and eating right make me feel good about myself. I rely on my own strength and health that I've developed over time and through hard work.

Leader: In order to feel secure in God's love, we must know and feel and experience the power of the Holy Spirit in our inner being. We must remove or cut out whatever "roots" or competitors get in the way of Christ feeling more and more at home in our hearts. We must believe that God loves us and reinforce this truth by the way that we treat ourselves and by the way that we treat one another. We must also become a group that prays for one another to understand the heights and depths of God's love until His love securely anchors us and until Christ's love freely flows in and out of our lives and relationships. We must dare to ask for more of His love, and dare to express more of His love to one another and to a world that desperately needs to know and feel and see God's love in action. *A group of people who are securely rooted in God's love can change the world!*

Facilitator:

- What lies, lifestyle patterns, or "old roots" are you willing to give up in order for our group to become the type of spiritual friends who are always ready to pray together, get together, and reach out together to touch our world with the Father's love?

- What is your biggest obstacle that you will need this group's prayer for and help with so that it does not get in the way of us being a loving community of friends? (The answer to this question is not "more time" or "more patience" or a change in someone else first.)

- If what we believe about ourselves and others determines how we relate to people, what do you currently believe about yourself? What do you currently believe about other people?

- Let's take Paul's prayer that we are studying and put it into our own words so that we can pray it over one another in our group.

26

I'll get you started, then go ahead and use the space to draft your own prayer.

Father, Because I can come to You with freedom and confidence,

_____

_____

_____

_____

_____

_____

_____

_____

_____

_____

_____ Amen.

TAKING THE NTD CHALLENGE

NTD level 1 challenge: If you want Christ to be more and more at home in your heart as you trust Him (but this is hard for you), read Robert Boyd Munger's short book *My Heart - Christ's Home* and discuss this with someone in our group (Munger).

NTD level 2 challenge: Take the prayer that you just wrote in your own words, and begin to pray it daily for the members of our NTD 2 group. Watch in expectation for God to answer your prayers.

Ephesians 3:14-21

NTD level 3 challenge: Ask someone in our group to come alongside you and journey with you through the stages of giving up "old roots" of an insecure foundation, while you are gradually replacing it with a more secure identity that is based on God's love and truth. This challenge may be best accomplished through a weekly outside-the-group contact that includes prayer time, opening God's Word together, and doing something together that you both enjoy (for example, drinking coffee, eating ice cream, scrapbooking, playing tennis, walking, playing games, shopping, working out, fishing).

Enjoy your challenge and keep your group posted on how you are coming along with the challenge(s) that you choose.

Ephesians 4:1-16
Growing up Together

Leader: Before we move into some ongoing discussions about building strong and healthy relationships, let's review the foundation that God has established for our relationships.

- God *loved* and *chose* us long before the foundations of this world.

- His unchanging plan has been to work through Jesus Christ to *adopt* us into His family as His very own children.

- God purchased our *freedom* from sin through Jesus' blood.

- When we believed in Christ, God *sealed* us as His very own by giving us His Holy Spirit, who lives in and through our lives.

- We have been *saved by grace* through our faith in Jesus Christ.

- We are God's *masterpiece*. He created us anew to do the good things He planned for us long ago.

- We can *fearlessly* come into God's presence and receive a *glad welcome.*

- We are *defined* and *deeply loved* by God.

When we know and believe these foundational truths, God calls us to live our lives in a way that consistently reflects these foundational truths. Who we are and whose we are define what we do and how we relate to one another as Christians. Let's read together Ephesians 4:1-6.

Facilitator:

- Why did Paul beg the church to life a life worthy of their calling (v. 1)?

29

Ephesians 4:1-16

- What are the six characteristics that describe how we are to live a life worthy of our calling (v. 2,3)?

- What do we have in common with other believers in the body of Christ (v. 4-6)?

- Who begs and challenges you to be more Christ-like in the way that you relate to people so that God may be glorified?

Leader: After Paul wrote to the church and reminded them of their foundation in Christ and their calling to be united, Paul described God's design for the church. Let's read together Ephesians 4:7-16.

The One who generously gave each of us gifts is the same One who rules and fills the universe. He's over us, in us, and working through us with the gifts that He's chosen to give us. God gave every believer a special gift, and He gave church leaders gifts and responsibilities to develop the church. Although the gifts vary, church leaders have the same responsibility. They are called by God to work together to *"equip God's people to do His work and build up the church"* (v. 12).

God's calling and gifting of church leaders comes with a huge responsibility. If you look closely at verse 13, you will learn the extent of church leaders' equipping and building-up responsibility for the church until we are *all* are:

- United in our faith and knowledge of Jesus Christ.

- Mature and fully-grown Christians.

- Measuring up to Christ's character.

Facilitator:

- Do you know what gifts that God has given you to help build up the church?

- What do you expect your pastors and teachers to be doing in your church?

- As we sometimes evaluate how pastors are doing at their calling, how many of the above three characteristics have you been committed to pursuing *with* the members of your church *under* your pastor's leadership?

Leader: By nature of being Christians--or Christ followers--we all gravitate toward different pathways of growth as we are becoming more Christ-like. Right? Actually, Satan is constantly trying to get us to believe his lies that get us off God's developmental path. In order for us to grow and mature as a Christian family, we must help one another *hold on to the truth in love.*

The process of growing into spiritual maturity is a Christ-led process. It is also a process where *each of us plays a vital role in developing the health and growth and love of one another.* We become more and more like Christ as we speak the truth in love and hold to the truth in love. If we truly love one another in our spiritual family, we will *not* ignore each other when we pursue:

- What is unhealthy.

- What causes our stagnation or destruction.

- Harmful relationship patterns.

Instead, *we will speak the truth in love and hold one another to the truth in love.* We may "catch some flak" for caring enough to confront our friends, but the alternative to loving is sitting back and watching our friends be duped by Satan into paths of destruction and saying nothing!

Facilitator:

- What are some of the ways that God has gifted you that help the church become more healthy, growing, and full of love?

- Can you share a recent example of how you have used your God-given gifts to help the church become healthier?

- When you are not okay, what are some ways that you contribute to the church being unhealthy, stagnating, or lacking love?

- Will you allow this group to become a place where we can speak the truth in love and hold one another to the truth in love? What would that look like in our group?

Leader: Jesus modeled for us how to be assertive in relationships. He confronted people with compassion. He assertively avoided temptations. He intentionally got away from people to pray to His Father. He directly addressed sin problems. He took action to respond to people in need. He raised the standards and addressed the truth and the needs behind the people's questions and behavior instead of giving in to what people wanted Him to say and do. Although some people would describe Jesus as radically assertive and counter-cultural, He also responded to conflicts with language and behaviors that we may describe as passive and aggressive. Therefore, we are not trying to build a case for Christian assertiveness. Instead, we are trying to learn what it means to speak the truth in love, to hold one another to the truth in love, and to do our part to help others grow.

We will be much better *positioned* to help one another grow and develop when we are taking the time to really get to know each other. Oftentimes, it is a matter of slowing down and making room in our schedules to be there for one another. When we make time to help one another in a practical way, it goes a long way. It involves more listening and responding instead of talking and controlling. When we position ourselves by praying with and for our friends, *God helps us discern what our role is to be in the ever-changing ebb and flow of our relationships.*

But most of us have not been trained to think in a "developmental model." We do not even think about what we need next in order to grow to become more like Christ. In fact, sometimes when you mention to people in the church that they need to do something differently to grow and develop, they give you the message, *"Leave me alone!"*

If you believe that we become more and more like Christ in every way as we know, live, share, speak, and hold to the truth in love, then why do we not see the growth and development of churches full of people who are being conformed to the image of Christ? In his book, *The Great Omission*, Dallas Willard has good insight into our problem.

"Most problems in contemporary churches can be explained by the fact that members have never decided to follow Christ" (Willard 5).

Facilitator: Let's take some time to complete the following statements:

- Christ-followers are people who...

- Christians who do not know or follow Christ's teachings and do not pass on these truths to those around them are...

- Jesus said that we are to make disciples and to teach them to obey everything...

TAKING THE NTD CHALLENGE

NTD level 1 challenge: Spend time in the gospels (Matthew, Mark, Luke, and John) this week exploring Jesus' teachings and commandments. Record what you discover about Jesus' teachings and what you discover about your own life.

_____

_____

_____

_____

_____

Ephesians 4:1-16

_____

_____

_____

_____

_____

NTD level 2 challenge: Schedule time this week with a friend. Share with them what you are learning about your roots and your relationships.

NTD level 3 challenge: Pick up a copy of Koch & Haugk's book, _Speaking the Truth in Love._ As you read through this book, begin to apply what you learn with a trusted friend. Caution: Applying what you learn in this book may take your relationships to a whole new level of adventure (Koch and Haugk).

Ephesians 4:17-32

Transformed by Christ

Facilitator: *(Bring enough hymnals to your group so that everyone has a copy.)* Let's begin our NTD 2 group by doing something different. Open your hymnal to the hymn "Take My Life, and Let It Be" (Take My Life, and Let It Be). Let's go around the group and read this hymn together out loud.

- What was your initial reaction to reading this hymn together?

- At what point in the hymn did you want to just stop and reflect on the words that were calling for more of your attention and demanded your response?

- Singing this prayer of consecration or transformation is one way of becoming set apart for Christ. What *tools* has God been using to reshape these parts of your life: your moments, your hands, your heart, your mind, your paths, your impulses, your words, your treasures, and your love?

Leader: This next passage of Scripture we are about to study is about *transformation*. It is about being changed by Christ. As we open our Bibles and read together Ephesians 4:17-32, let's prepare ourselves to hear God's Word and to allow God to transform us through His Word.

Leaders are readers, and if you spend much time reading the Bible, devotional books, and leadership articles, you know that "transformation" is a hot topic and a complex process. But as we explore God's Word, keep in mind some important principles regarding transformation:

- God and His Word do not change.

35

Ephesians 4:17-32

- We tend to resist changes that require deep change on our part. In other words, we are not very good at making changes ourselves.

- We cannot change others. And if we try to change others, we will likely get frustrated and create conflicts in our relationships.

- God is the One who transforms us from the inside out. We can cooperate with this process, or we can resist His methods of growing us to become more like Christ. The more we resist God, the more His methods of helping us grow may become increasingly painful.

- We do not grow in isolation. We need one another to grow in maturity, health, and love. (Ephesians 4:16b)

Facilitator: Let's slowly walk through this passage (Ephesians 4:17-32) and identify the changes that are to gradually occur in us as we allow God to transform us:

- How closely we are to follow the life of God.

- What we do with our old nature and former way of living.

- Our heart.

- Our thoughts and attitudes.

- Our nature.

- Who we become like.

- What we say (how we say it) and what we do not say.

- What we do.

- What we do with our emotions.

- How we work.

- Our lifestyle.

- Who we live for.

- What we get rid of.

- How we treat one another.

God wants to use every part of our lives to transform us into His likeness and to use every part of our lives to contribute to others becoming more like Christ.

- The previous statement is another way of describing "discipleship." As you reflect on your life, where are you in the *process* of growing to become more like Jesus?

- What obstacles are you currently facing that slow down the process of becoming more like Christ?

- How is your life contributing to others becoming more like Christ?

Leader: In his book *The Disciple-Making Pastor*, Bill Hull wrote:

"Jesus stated the Great Commission the way He did, because 'make disciples of all nations' means much more than 'make converts of all nations.' Only healthy disciples reproduce. If the church fails to make disciples, it fails to multiply. If the church fails to multiply, it fails." (Hull 133)

Facilitator:

- Are we becoming healthy disciples of Jesus Christ?

- What are the signs that we're reproducing healthy Christ-followers?

- We are reproducing our lives. Those around us are becoming more…

Ephesians 4:17-32

- How is the church making healthy disciples that reproduce?

- How is the church failing to multiply?

Leader: These questions are difficult to answer, and many churches are trying to discover the answers to these questions. However, many churches, and many small groups, are not even asking these questions. They are busy doing what they have always been doing, or they might be out trying the newest, latest thing that all of the other "successful" churches are doing. *How long would you go to a church that failed to change lives and failed to change the surrounding community?*

Transformation of churches and communities begins when pastors, church leaders, small groups, and people position themselves for spiritual formation. Spiritual formation is a gradual process of allowing God to remake us into what He intended us to be like: conformed to the image of Christ—for the benefit of others. Paul introduced us to the process of spiritual formation:

"Therefore, I urge you brothers, in view of God's mercy, to offer your bodies as living sacrifices, holy and pleasing to God—this is your spiritual act of worship. Do not conform any longer to the pattern of this world, but be transformed by the renewing of your mind. Then you will be able to test and approve what God's will is—His good, pleasing and perfect will" (Romans 12:1, 2 NIV).

But reading these Scriptures and identifying what God wants to change in us is not the same as transformation. *We must be careful* not to confuse studying the process of transformation with real change and transformation.

Changing and growing to become more like Christ individually, and as a small group, takes years of practice, obedience, commitment, consistency, accountability, sacrifice, denying self, nonconformity to the cultural patterns of this world, and support. It involves moving from a position of what I want or what we want to a position of *what God wants* from our

38

lives or from our group. It involves making more time and more room in our lives for God, for spiritual disciplines, for serving, and for one another. Growing up together spiritually will require each of us to take God, His Word, ourselves, and each other more seriously. We must become a united, growing family of Christ-followers who are invested in each other's lives and invested together in making Christ known in practical ways in our community.

In order to become healthy, reproducing disciples, we must become more honest with and about ourselves with God and with one another. Instead of avoiding conflicts and staying in our comfort zones, we must learn to speak the truth in love with one another and create opportunities that will contribute to deepening our devotion to God and to one another's spiritual growth. This will require change on the part of each of us, and it will require a deeper level of knowing, loving, and connectedness than we probably have at this point.

As you begin to reflect on what it may require of you for us to grow together spiritually, some may be saying "yes" inside, while others may be saying "No, this is not what I am looking for." But if we are to be a group where we each do our part to help the other parts grow in maturity, health, and love, then we must have a mutual commitment to one another's growth and development as Christ-followers.

TAKING THE NTD CHALLENGE

NTD level 1 challenge: In Ephesians 4:17, we are admonished to ***"Live no longer as the ungodly do."*** This is a serious God-challenge to be radically different from those around you. Take some time this week to meet with someone from our NTD 2 group and share with them some of the ways that God is transforming your life as you are following Jesus. Discuss how you're responding to God's challenge to live

Ephesians 4:17-32

differently.   Here is a place to journal some spiritual reflections from your conversations together.

_____

_____

_____

_____

NTD level 2 challenge: Spend some time alone with God in today's passage of Scripture (Ephesians 4:17-32). Ask God what areas of your life that He wants to transform during this next season of your spiritual journey. Here is a place to record what God places on your heart.

_____

_____

_____

_____

NTD level 3 challenge: Set up a time to meet with someone from our NTD 2 group. When you meet together, share with them the areas of your life that you believe God wants to transform. Ask them for their help, feedback, prayers, support, and accountability during the process of transformation. Here is a place to record what you want to share with your supportive friend and how they responded to you.

_____

_____

_____

_____

Remember that any growth and change that God makes in and through our lives is for the benefit of others and for the glory of God.

Ephesians 5:1-20
Imitating Christ

Leader: When you read the Bible, what questions frequently come to your mind? Do you ever just stop what you are reading and ask God your questions? God knows our questions before we ask them. He wants us to come to Him with our questions, seeking answers. He's given us inquiring minds to discover His truth. If you have ever had the privilege to sit under Howard Hendricks' teaching, he would frequently say, "Bombard the text with questions" (Hendricks 39).

Today, as we begin to explore Ephesians 5:1-2, you may recognize some of your questions. You may also be challenged by His answers. Here we go...

- *"Follow God's example"* (v. 1a)
  (When and Where?)

- *"in everything you do"* (v. 1b)
  (Why?)

- *"because you are His dear children."* (v. 1c)
  (How?)

- *"Live a life filled with love for others"* (v. 2a)
  (What will that look like?)

- *"following the example of Christ"* (v. 2b)
  (How did He do it?)

- *"who loved you and gave Himself as a sacrifice to take away your sins."* (v. 2c)
  (What will loving and giving look like when we are doing it as Christ did?)

41

Ephesians 5:1-20

Sounds like good questions and a logical progression. So why do we have problems in and between us? Problems arise in and between us when we follow God's example *some of the time*. Problems arise when we try to follow God's example, but we are not sure that we are His dear children. Problems arise when we are not sure of who He is, who we are, or whose we are. Problems arise when we try to live a life filled with love for others when we do not really feel loved by God or feel loved by others. And problems arise in and between us when our lives are organized around serving self instead of loving and giving to others.

Facilitator:

- What process is God using to help you become more like Jesus?

- How much of a difference does it make in your life that you are a *dear child of God*?

- When do you feel loved by God?

- What makes it hard for you to grasp that you are *God's masterpiece*?

- Does loving and giving sacrificially flow out of your life to others? Or do you have to "work at getting outside of yourself" to love and give sacrificially to others?

Leader: You may wonder why there are so many reflection questions built into this NTD 2 group. Why are the questions so personal? It has a lot to do with *valuing the process* of developing the strong, healthy root system of our identity, our worldview, and our relationships. As we are developing a deeper relationship with our Creator, we discover and feel Jesus' deep love for us; we discover His purpose and plan for our lives; and we allow God to transform us to become more like Jesus in order to become healthy disciple-makers for God. *Without a clear understanding of who God is, who we are, and God's mission for our lives, there is no strong or healthy motivation to become imitators of Christ.* In fact, *"most churched and unchurched Christians live by the 'great omission' instead of living by the 'Great Commission.'"* (Willard 21-22) Maybe we should read this again and take time to respond before we move on with our study. *(pause for reflection and engage in spirited discussion)*

As we read together Ephesians 5:3-20, pay close attention to the *commandments* and *contrasts* that you hear as we allow God's Spirit to define what it looks like to imitate Christ.

What are we being called to do as we are imitating Christ?

- Be _____. (5:4b)

- Let our behavior be a clear reflection of God's _____. (5:8)

- Discover what is _____ to the Lord. (5:10)

- Be careful to live _____. (5:15)

- Make the most of every opportunity to do _____ in these evil days. (5:16)

- Let the Holy Spirit _____ and _____ you. (5:18)

- Sing, make music, and give thanks to God for _____. (5:19,20)

What are we being commanded *not* to do as we are imitating Christ?

- Be sexually immoral, impure, or _____. (5:3)

- Tell obscene stories, use foolish talk, or tell coarse _____. (5:4)

- Be fooled by people who excuse these _____ (5:6) or participate in the things these people do.

- Take part in _____ _____ of evil and darkness. (5:11)

- Talk about the things _____ people do in secret. (5:12)

- Act without _____. (5:17)

Ephesians 5:1-20

- Get _____ because it will ruin your life. (5:18)

Do you like the way that Paul sums up what it means to follow God's example in everything you do because you are His dear children?

"So be careful how you live, not as fools, but as those who are wise" (Ephesians 5:15).

In an age when our church is saturated with "tolerance," casual, come-as-you-are "worship," consumerism, marital unfaithfulness, leadership crises, and "wild-at-heart" Christians who dress, act, and relate like the world, Paul's message to the church seems to be as relevant as ever. *Be careful how you speak and live.* For those who follow and imitate Christ are equally concerned with what we do as well as what we do *not* do.

In his book, *The Great Omission*, Dallas Willard helps Christians to understand that *in order to live the life God made us for, we must learn three crucial lessons from Jesus.*

1. We must learn from Jesus the reason why we do what we do. As we trust Jesus and take up His cause, He teaches us how to make the right choices that glorify Him.

2. Jesus wants to replace our inner character (guts, insides) with His heart, character, and eyes so that we see and respond to God and people as He would. This process gradually occurs as we follow Jesus into the practice of spiritual disciplines.

3. Jesus wants our lives to be in sync and in cooperation with His Spirit as He daily interacts with us and with the people who surround us. As we expect Jesus' involvement and as we attend to and participate in what He is doing in our midst, we help those around us to join in. (Willard 20-22)

Facilitator: Let's take some time to unpack and respond to what we have been learning today.

- How much time and attention do you give to Jesus' life and teachings? When are you intentional about imitating Jesus?

- What is one change that you could make that would position you to become an apprentice, a student, or one who is learning to become more and more like Jesus?

- Pick one of Willard's three lessons that Jesus wants to teach us and respond to it with our group.

TAKING THE NTD CHALLENGE

Today's group will end with a good challenge: Intentionally seek out someone you know who imitates Christ in their life. Spend time with them, and ask them to share with you the process that God has been taking them through that has resulted in other people seeing Christ in them. Use the space below to record your experience and what you learned.

_____

_____

_____

_____

_____

_____

_____

_____

_____

_____

Ephesians 5:1-20

_____

_____

_____

_____

_____

_____

_____

_____

Ephesians 5:21-33
Spirit-Guided Relationships

Facilitator: As we begin today's NTD 2 group, let's take some time to share some of the good things that came from last week's NTD 2 challenge.

Leader: Although our group takes breaks between lessons, it is important to realize that the subtitles and breaks built into our common day Bibles were not part of the original Greek language of the New Testament scrolls. We'll reflect back on the flow of thought from our last group.

We are going to explore what a marriage looks like when both spouses are following God's example in everything they do, living a life filled with love, being careful to make the most of every opportunity to do good, not acting thoughtlessly, trying to understand what the Lord wants them to do, and allowing the Holy Spirit to fill and control them.

Now that we are moving into the flow of thought, and we are getting mentally prepared for what God is about to teach us about what a biblical marriage looks like, look what comes next in the passage:

"And further, you will submit to one another out of reverence for Christ" (Ephesians 5:21).

Now there may be many men, women, and pastors who have not made this thesis statement central to their understanding of what it means to have a biblical marriage. Most people have not been taught or observed mutual yielding and submission modeled in a healthy marriage. Nowadays, it is probably more common for children to grow up in a broken home because there was not mutual submission between their parents. Or it is more likely for one spouse to be more dominant or

47

controlling. How often have you heard the phrase, "Well, we know who wears the pants in that family!"

Reader: Let's explore God's design for a Christian marriage as we read together Ephesians 5:21-33.

Facilitator:

- What are some of the *characteristics* you heard or read in this passage of Scripture that described a *Christian marriage*?

- Why do so many husbands come home after a long day of work and become *couch potatoes* instead of looking for ways to *serve* their wife and children?

- Although most *men* want things to go their own way at home, God designed a husband's role to be one who gives up his life to love, serve, and make his wife look really good. Jesus gave men a living model of *serving, sacrificing love* to follow so that men would know how to serve their wives. These next questions are just for the married men in our group.

  o Have you discovered what your wife's "love language" is? *(What makes her really look good and feel loved?)* (Chapman)

  o Would you say her "love tank" is full, half full, or almost on empty? (Chapman)

- You may have experienced a peaceful home at times when the *wife* is content. She gracefully submits to her husband's leadership as he is following God's leadership in the home. But there are also times when women have a harder time submitting to their husbands. Women, can you talk about why *submitting* to your husband "in everything" is a challenging biblical command to obey?

- Part of what helps a marriage become healthy is having two healthy spouses who have separated themselves from their family of origin. What happens to a marriage when the wife and/or the husband *fail to set good boundaries* with their families of origin?

- What *process* does God's Spirit lead us through to help us learn to submit to God and to submit to one another?

- "Submitting" and "loving with the same love that Christ showed the church" may look an awful lot *alike* in a healthy marriage. What are some of the ways that Christ submitted and loved?

- When you look closely at the biblical text, "submission" and "loving" in marriage are both commands. They are not two options if you have time, if you have energy, or if you feel like it. When you take Christ at His Word by serving and loving your spouse, *what will your spouse notice?*

- When is it hard for wives to love and submit to their husbands in everything?

- When is it easy for wives to love and submit to their husbands in everything?

- How can two be united into one? Practicing biblical unity in marriage is *real* when you share your life, body, time, decisions, space, faith, dreams, remote controls, tools, music, money, vehicle(s), children, phone(s), feelings, thoughts, and so much more. How would you complete the following sentence: *"It has been hard for me to share my _____ in my marriage."*

Leader: One of the main reasons why marriages crumble is because *spouses retain control* and have not given up "their _____" in order for the two to become one. This lack of surrender, submission, or unity is frequently caused by a *damaged ability to trust* one another. Rather than inviting Jesus Christ to heal our trust wounds, we are more prone to keep more to ourselves and share less in marriage. "Control conflicts" and

Ephesians 5:21-33

"disunity" may better describe many of our marriages than "two becoming one."

But how many of our marital struggles are the result of just plain selfishness? *I like to have my own way...* In the bedroom. In the kitchen. With the TV or computer. Where I go out to eat. Who comes over to my house. How much money I spend on what. How I make decisions. How I fold the clothes. When and where and if I go to church.

There comes a turning point in the life of a church or small group when we must turn the corner on the marriage and divorce crisis, and we must learn to obey Christ's teaching by bearing with one another in brotherly and sisterly love. Although it may feel somewhat awkward or uncomfortable letting others really get to know us, our marriages may become much healthier when we reach out for help and support. Sometimes speaking or hearing the unvarnished truth about the way our marriage really is will help us learn to love and be there more for one another at a deeper level. Responding to the following challenges may also help strengthen our marriages.

TAKING THE NTD CHALLENGE

NTD level 1 challenge: If you are married, make some time with your spouse to discuss ways that you can practice love and godly submission in your marriage. See how many different ways you can love and serve one another over the next week. (Husbands: Make sure your wife does not out-serve you!)

NTD level 2 challenge: Whether you are single or married, make some time to get together with a married couple from our group. While you are together, pay attention to the different ways that the married couple loves and serves one another. Give them some positive feedback from your observations.

Ephesians 6:1-9

Family Matters

Leader: Imagine that you are a part of a family that has taken God's Word to heart. You have applied Paul's biblical teaching to your life and family. You recognize and affirm that God has loved and chosen each of your family members as His very own. You have received God's special favor, and you treat one another as God's masterpiece. Jesus Christ is the cornerstone of your family. You enjoy the privilege of sharing God's good news with people. Christ is becoming more and more at home in your heart as your identity is becoming deeply rooted in the enduring love of Christ. You speak the truth in love, and you practice mutual submission with your spouse. You are following Christ's example of living a life filled with love while making the most of every opportunity to do good as the Holy Spirit leads you.

Facilitator:

- What was it like trying to imagine being part of a family like this? Some may just laugh. Some may say, "Yeah, right! Get real!" Some may think this is way too idealistic to even consider living in a family like this. Others may be striving and longing to be part of a Christ-centered, loving family.

- What words would you use to describe your family?

- How hard would it be for children and teens to obey their parents if their parents practiced sacrificial love and mutual submission?

- Let's read together Ephesians 6:1-4.

Leader: There are no guarantees that children will obey their parents because it is the right thing to do. How long would it take you to think

51

of a time when you disobeyed your parents when you were growing up? *What came to your mind when you took a quick stroll down childhood memory lane?*

Even though children know that they are supposed to obey their parents for all of the right reasons, it just is not that easy. Many parents and children feel disconnected and have a hard time making time for one another. Children, and many times parents, live for the moment without considering one another's feelings, plans, or preferences. Words like "obey", "honor", and "blessing" are not usually spoken in most homes. You might even be hard-pressed to find intact families with parents and children who submit, love, listen, and are there for each other. It would be easier to find families with an absent parent, unsupervised kids, parents who ignore or annoy their children, and children or teens who mouth off to their parents and ignore what their parents tell them to do.

But if you listen carefully, you might hear a cry from people who are looking for a spiritual father and spiritual mother, people who will take seriously your life and faith questions and teach you how to understand and apply God's Word to daily life and family living. You may be one of those people who are looking for a spiritual mentor. Or you may have people looking to you for spiritual guidance and direction.

Becoming spiritually mature is an extremely long and difficult process. It requires a long obedience to God in the same direction. It involves a willingness to take seriously God, His Word, yourself, and those around you. If we dare to take God at His Word and take daily steps to learn and apply Christ's teaching to our life and relationships, our family will notice, and they will feel like they matter more to us.

"Submitting" and "listening" will become benchmarks in the process of maturing spiritually. Submitting to Christ and His plan for our lives involves a daily dying to ourselves and doing what He wants us to do. Our family members will notice that we care more about discovering what God's purpose is for their lives. Spiritual growth will also be an outgrowth of surrounding ourselves with godly people who invest in our spiritual development. Good spiritual leaders make time and do whatever it takes to help others grow and develop personally and spiritually.

Facilitator:

- Who do you trust your heart with to help you grow and mature as a Christ-follower?

- Who looks to you for spiritual leadership?

- Are you making time each day to spiritually nurture those whom God has placed around your life?

- What do you say and do that irritates and angers your family members?

- Are you willing to stop being a thorn in their flesh?

- Were you raised by godly parents who brought you up in the discipline and instruction approved by God?

- What "discipline" and "instruction" is approved by God?

Leader: Ephesians 6:5-9 emphasizes how slaves and masters should treat one another. In this passage we learn the importance of working with all of our heart for God and treating people as God's masterpieces. We should show each person God's love and favor.

Facilitator:

- Can you think of a time when you were working for someone and you were conscious of the fact that you were working for the Lord and not working for the other person?

- Do you currently work for people whom you deeply respect? Do you serve them sincerely and with enthusiasm as you would serve Christ?

Ephesians 6:1-9

Leader: As we are coming closer to the end of this NTD 2 group, you may have a growing understanding of the connection between the strength of your spiritual roots and the quality of your significant relationships. The more you nurture the development of your spiritual roots, the more you will nurture and care about the spiritual roots and lives of your loved ones.

TAKING THE NTD CHALLENGE
Creative Exercise

Option #1—Draw a picture of our NTD 2 group using trees. Imagine that we are trees growing together. Carve the name of each person in our group in the tree that represents them. Draw trees for each of our family members. Draw which of our trees (relationships) are more closely connected and which of our trees are more distant. Draw the root system of each tree. Write on the roots where you see each one trying to get their life from. Draw fruit on the trees that seem to be bearing fruit. Write on the fruit what you see their lives and relationships bearing. Somewhere in the trees or forest, give your tree community a name that defines our group. When you're finished drawing, share your drawing with the group and ask for their feedback.

Option #2—Draw a picture of our NTD 2 group using a building. Incorporate into your drawing some of the teaching and messages that you have been internalizing as we have been studying Ephesians together as a community of friends. Be sure to include the foundation stones or blocks. Write on the blocks of our building the truths that anchor and connect us as a faith community. Once you have concluded drawing our building, determine whether the door of our lives (building) is truly open and welcoming to have others join us or if the door of our lives is more closed to "outsiders." Grab a marker and write some graffiti on the walls of our building (what you imagine someone on the outside of our group might say about us). In one of the rooms of our building, write a message that you're been wrestling with. On the front of the building, give our building a name that accurately defines what our group is becoming. Feel free to include any other aspects you'd like to personalize our building. When you're finished drawing, share your drawing with the group and ask for their feedback.

Prayer: Lord, Thanks for helping us to find new ways to connect and express ourselves as we are becoming Your church. Keep growing and building us together until we reflect You well to the world. Amen.

Ephesians 6:1-9

Ephesians 6:10-24
Standing Strong Together

Leader: Whether you are on the last lap of a big race, in the fourth quarter of the game, or in the last season of your ministry and life, we all hope to finish well and leave a legacy for others to follow. And the Apostle Paul's life and legacy was no exception. He understood the battle, the enemy, and the challenge. Therefore, Paul, our spiritual battalion leader, closed his letter with some wise and powerful words of caution and preparation as we embark upon our spiritual battlefields. Let's read together Ephesians 6:10-24.

Paul concluded his letter with a strong message to his spiritual battalion as they were gearing up for a long spiritual war. His message was clear: **"Be strong with the Lord's mighty power"** (v. 10). But then Paul broke his message down into three parts:

- Put on *all* of God's armor so that you will be able to stand firm against *all* of the strategies and *all* of the tricks of Satan. Paul knew that in order to stand strong in battle, *we must know our enemy* and understand the enemy's warfare tactics.

- If you want to remain standing strong after your battle, *you must know and use every piece of God's armor* so that you can resist the enemy.

- *Pray* continually on every occasion in the power of the Holy Spirit.

Facilitator:

- Describe a spiritual battle that you have *won*. Discuss the armor and weapons that you used to stand firm and win the battle.

57

Ephesians 6:10-24

- Describe a spiritual battle that you have *lost*. Discuss the places that your armor was incomplete (vulnerable places) and ways that your weapons were not sharpened for battle.

- What are you learning about your enemy Satan? What does Satan know about you that is hard for you to admit?

- Can each of you *define each piece of God's armor* and how it helps you resist the enemy and stand firm in battle?

- What role does *prayer* play in your life as you are involved in spiritual battlefields?

- If you tied together the spiritual wisdom that God communicated through Paul's letter to the Ephesian church, how would you put it into your own words? *(pause for your group members to share their responses.)*

Leader: Paul put it this way: Know that God has been working throughout history to accomplish His plan and purpose. His unchanging plan was to adopt us into His own family, bringing us to Himself through Jesus Christ. He purchased our freedom through the blood of Christ and showered us with all wisdom and understanding.

Out of His great love, grace, and favor, God saved us when we believed in Jesus Christ. In God's eyes, we are His masterpiece, created anew in Jesus Christ to do the good things that He planned for us long ago. And the more we become rooted and filled with Christ's love, the more it will overflow into our relationships at home, with other members of God's family, and with those who do not yet believe in Jesus Christ.

As we are learning to love one another like Christ loves us, our behavior in relationships will demonstrate humility, gentleness, patience, forbearance, and unity. As we are each developing and using our God-given gifts and talents, we are becoming stronger Christians and a strong Christian family. As we are speaking the truth in love and each one is doing his/her special part, we are becoming healthier and more full of God's love.

Our roots and relationships become increasingly strong and healthy as we put off the old self, and as we become spiritually renewed in our thoughts, attitudes, and behavior towards one another. The more we allow God's Spirit to permeate our lives, the more He allows us to love one another and make the most of our daily opportunities to do good to one another.

The strength of our spiritual roots will be most accurately displayed in our relationships with our family members. You can tell a lot about a person's character and faith by the way they think about, speak to, and treat their family members. When God's truths become wedded with loving words and actions, your faith will be attractive to your family, friends, and neighbors.

Maybe that is why Satan is constantly attacking our hearts through our homes. He wants to discourage and defeat us. He wants to distract and disarm us. His "strategies and tricks" take many forms. But when we allow his tactics to keep us from being vigilant in prayer and connected to His family, our armor begins to drop, and we do not even recognize it.

That is why we need God, His Word, and each another to be strong and healthy. We need to speak the truth in love and occasionally hear the unvarnished truth about our lives and relationships. We each need to discover and do our part so that God's family becomes a strong and healthy group that His Spirit uses to communicate His eternal, life-changing truths to a world that desperately needs to see and discover His love.

Facilitator: As we come to the close of this NTD 2 group, let's take some time to reflect on some important issues that we are facing.

Ephesians 6:10-24

- What keeps you from having an identity that is deeply rooted in Christ's enduring love?

- What pathways lead to your feeling disconnected from God and from the people who love you?

- Will you allow the people in this group to have enough of your time so that we can get to know and love you the way God uniquely made you?

- How much time and energy will you invest in getting to know and love the people that God has placed in our NTD 2 group? *The best way to spell love is still T-I-M-E.*

- Before concluding today's group, will you please take a few minutes to complete the NTD 2 evaluation and return it to your group leader. Thank you.

NTD 2 EVALUATION

<u>Facilitator</u>:   Before concluding this group, let's journal our thoughts/feelings prompted by the questions below as we reflect upon our NTD 2 experiences. Then we will make time to discuss some of our reflections with the group.

As we studied Ephesians together as a group, I discovered that God...

As we studied Ephesians together as a group, I discovered that I...

Some of the important things I learned about my identity are...

Through our NTD 2 group I learned that my relationships are...

NTD 2 Evaluation

This small group experience for me was…

What I liked about NTD 2 was…

What I disliked about NTD 2 was...

The structure and process of NTD 2 allowed me to…

The content and questions of NTD 2 were…

If someone asked me about NTD 2, I would tell them…

WORKS CITED

Chapman, Gary. *The 5 Love Languages*. Chicago: Northfield Publishing, 2015.

Gaither, William J. "I am A Promise." 1975. Sheet Music.

Havergal, Frances R. "Take My Life, and Let It Be." 1874. Hymn.

Hendricks, Howard. *Living by the Book*. Chicago: Moody Press, 1991.

Hull, Bill. *The Disciple-Making Pastor: Leading Others on the Journey of Faith*. Grand Rapids: Baker Books, 2007. Print.

Hutchcraft, Ron. *5 Needs Your Child Must Have Met at Home*. Grand Rapids: Zondervan, 1995. Print.

Koch, Ruth N. and Kenneth C. Haugk. *Speaking the Truth in Love*. St. Louis: Stephen Ministries, 1992. Print.

Manning, Brennan. *A Glimpse of Jesus: The Stranger to Self-Hatred*. New York: HarperOne, 2004. Print.

—. *Ruthless Trust*. New York: Doubleday and Company, 2000.

Munger, Boyd. *My Heart - Christ's Home*. Westmont: IVP Books, 2001. Print.

Willard, Dallas. *The Great Omission*. New York: HarperOne, 2006. Print.

Made in the USA
Columbia, SC
06 February 2021